To Sal
New opp...
coming your way.
Call in the Angels to
help manage your time
and energies so that
abundance can be yours.
Blessings
Netty

Angels for Life

By Netty

Find the answers to your life questions through this Angel channelled book of discovery.

1

Published 2007 by arima publishing

www.arimapublishing.com

ISBN 978-1-84549-188-8

Printed and bound in the United Kingdom

Typeset in Palatino Linotype 12/16

swirl is an imprint of arima Publishing

arima publishing
ASK House, Northgate Avenue
Bury St Edmunds, Suffolk IP32 6BB
t: (+44) 01284 700321

www.arimapublishing.com

Thanks

I would firstly like to thank my Spirit Guide Kay and the Angels for choosing me to produce such a powerful book. I only wish that I could produce the artwork with my eyes open!

I would also like to thank my family and friends especially Karl, Joanne, Phil, Jason, Tove, Marie, Falc, David, Wendy, Sue, Barbara and Nick for supporting me throughout my spiritual work. Special thanks must go to my Mum and Dad who undertook the task of typesetting all the pages of channelled text from the automatic writings of the Angels, which was not easy as all the Angels have very different styles of handwriting!

To Jack, Hannah and Olivia my three very special children. I hope as your Mum, I have given you the roots to know who you are and the wings to be free to be who you want to be.

Wishing you all love, light and laughter always.

Netty x

For Kay

Kay is my spirit guide, this photograph shows her as an orb in which you can see her face.

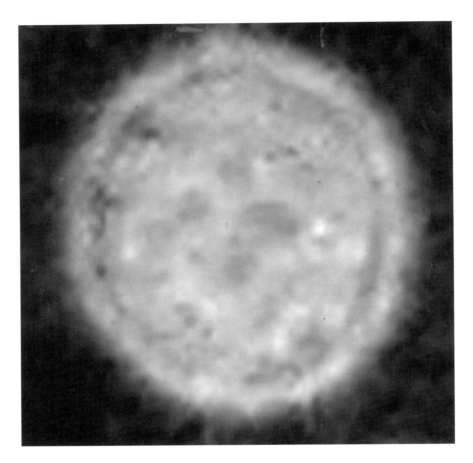

Angels for Life

About the book

The artwork and interpretations in this book were produced in trance by connecting to the Angels.

How to use the book

First ground yourself by imagining tree roots coming from the soles of your feet, growing deep into the earth. As you imagine the roots going deeper and deeper into the earth, your feet will start to feel heavier or will have a change of sensation in some way.

Next close your eyes and concentrate on the question you want answering.

When you are ready open a page of the book and read the channelled message under the appropriate heading, go straight to the Yes or No answer, or simply gaze at the psychic artwork to receive your own personal message. Each time you look at the pictures you may see different aspects. The pictures can be viewed from all angles and the first answers that you have in your mind will be the right answer for you.

This is a powerful book, which can be used for personal readings and guidance or for giving readings to other people. It can be used daily to receive your messages from spirit and the Angels by asking the question "What are my messages today?" or by asking specific questions, where a solution needs to be found.

FANTASY

The fantasy image is asking you to get in touch with your inner child, you have forgotten how to laugh and have fun. Ask the Angels and your guides how to rekindle the childlike qualities that you have within you, so that you can start to enjoy life again. Look closely at the picture and you will see your fantasy castle nestling amongst the clouds.

LOVE

You seem to want the fairytale romance. If you spend most of your time dreaming about what you want in a relationship then you will miss the opportunity to find lasting love. Wake up and you will see that the relationship you want is around you.

CAREER

You are right you can do better, stay focused on the outcome you desire and your dreams will become a reality.

FINANCES

Caution is needed at the moment as you are going through a period when you need to save rather than spend, be strict with yourself and you will see your finances stabilise and in a short while money is attracted to you as if by magic.

YES or NO   No

Archangel Michael brought this message to you.

BODY

Slow down and listen to your body and mind, it is urging you to spend more time in quiet mediation or prayer, so that you can listen to your inner guidance without interference from the outside world. When you do this your mind, spirit and body will feel more balanced. Look closely at the image and you will see your heart Chakra.

LOVE
Stay true to your heart; you know there is a soul connection between you.

CAREER
Stop letting other people put you down with their words and actions, take time to explore what you really want to do in your life.

FINANCES
The Universe is about to reward you over the coming months, get ready to receive abundance. Ask and you shall receive needs to be your affirmation at this time in your life.

YES or NO   Yes

Archangel Raphael has brought this message to you.

CHANGE

The images show that lighter and brighter times are ahead for you and your loved ones. The Angels know that you have been through some rough times and are answering your prayers.

LOVE
Hold in there, you will see things improve and you will know what you have to do, simply wait, think then act. Things are not as bad as they seem.

CAREER
New opportunities or a promotion is coming your way.

FINANCES
Money will be steady so try not to waste it for the next month.

YES or NO   Yes

Emmanuel brought this message to you.

LIGHT

You are about to embark on the next step along your spiritual journey.

All your intuitive gifts will be heightened at this time. Talk to your Angels and guides and they will assist you. Read more, attend courses with like-minded people and watch yourself grow spiritually. In the image the light is ever flowing, this represents the abundance of help for you and your soul's journey.

LOVE
Concentrate on the positive and not the negative, you are blessed and beautiful but sometimes you forget it.

CAREER
Now is the time to show people what you can really do. Work to your true potential and you will reap the rewards.

FINANCES
You are about to enter a lucky period of your life so any investments at this stage could become fruitful.

YES or NO   Yes

Archangel Michael brought this message to you.

OBSTACLES

You have overcome many obstacles in your life but the Angels and the white healing light of protection have protected you. If you stay focused on what you really want you will see that the way ahead gets easier.

LOVE
You are seeing problems that are not there, so stop blaming others.

CAREER
A choice will have to be made regarding your career over the coming months, ask yourself this question: Does it really serve you a purpose anymore?

FINANCES
Finances are improving so try not to worry.

YES or NO   No

Israfel brought this message to you.

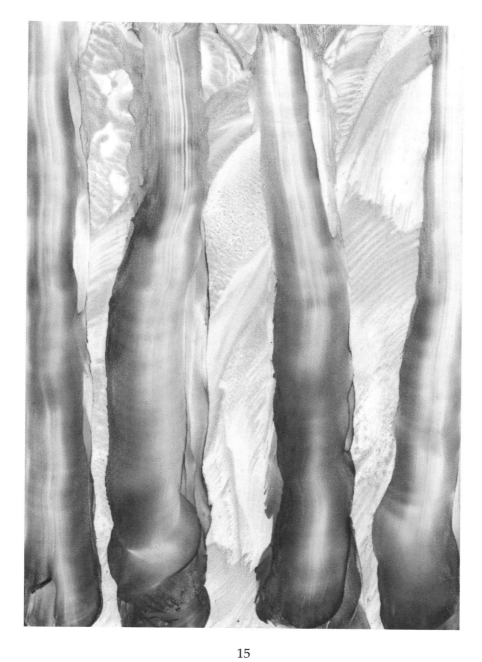

COMPASSION

Stand true to your beliefs and faith, have empathy and compassion towards others. They are on their journey too. When you look closely at the image you may see a face: What messages and thoughts spring into your mind?

LOVE
You are very much loved at this time; try to express how you really feel to ensure that you are not giving out mixed signals.

CAREER
Try not to get involved with problems that do not concern you.

FINANCES
Concentrate on what you have, rather than what you do not have at this present time.

YES or NO   Yes

Cassiel brought this message to you.

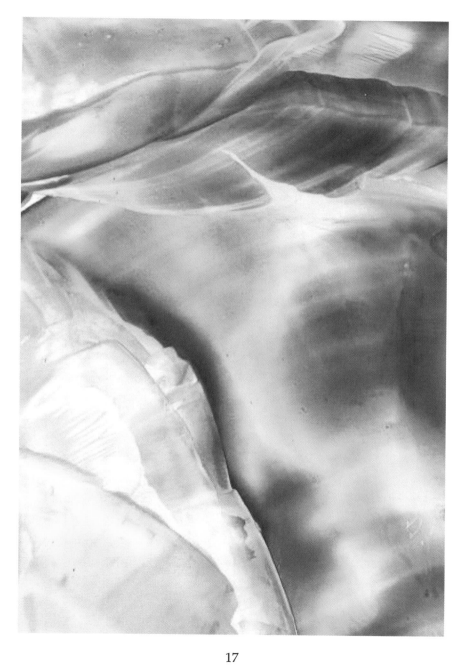

ANGELS

The Angels are with you at this time; so do not forget to ask them for help. Archangel Michael is working with you to give you courage to make the necessary changes in your life. Look out for white feathers, as these will be your sign that your prayers have been heard.

LOVE
You do not love yourself as much as you should, you have been hurt in the past and the Angels are healing this hurt. Look to the future and not the past.

CAREER
You are being guided into a role, which will serve you well.

FINANCES
Watch out for an unexpected bill that will need your immediate attention.
The Angels want you to be prepared.

YES or NO   No

Archangel Michael brought this message to you.

HOPE

You are in a situation and you feel there is no solution. You have forgotten about hope. Restore hope into your thinking and you will see a positive outcome.

LOVE
Manifest what you really want concerning your love life, make sure you are specific and then ask the universe to provide for you.

CAREER
Look to new areas of study to get the job that you really want.

FINANCES
Improvement will be made within the coming months. Use your finances wisely as you have let money slip through your fingers in the past and you have had very little to show for it. Only purchase things that you need rather than what you want.

YES or NO   Yes

Gabriel brought this message to you.

WATER

Connect again with Water as your mind, body and spirit needs to feel refreshed. Drink, play and relax in water to give you the energy you require at this time.

LOVE
Accept the changes that are happening in your love life and go with it. If water stands still, it becomes stagnant. When water is flowing the energies are playful and refreshing - This is like relationships.

CAREER
You will hear good news connected to your career within the coming weeks.

FINANCES
Only buy what you need and no more at this time. Too many commitments may make your journey slower but you will still be making progress.

YES or NO   No

Tabriss brought this message to you.

EMERGING

Look how far you have come on your journey. You are like the butterfly opening its wings for the first time, you have all that you need to take flight and see the beauty of the world.

LOVE
You will get the commitment and security you deserve but it will happen in divine timing.

CAREER
Go for it! A new opportunity will attract your attention; you have everything to gain from exploring it.

FINANCES
Resist the temptation to borrow money.

YES or NO   Yes

Zadkiel brought this message to you.

WAIT

Why are you in such a rush? You don't have to make any decisions at this time.
Wait and only make your next move when you are confident that you are in possession of the
full facts.

LOVE
Your instincts are right, think carefully before you make a decision that you may later regret.

CAREER
You are feeling under valued at the moment but this feeling will pass.

FINANCES
You have the power to attract money to you at this time. Look for the signs that the Angels
and your guides are showing you.

YES or NO   No

Archangel Michael brought this message to you.

COMFORT ZONE

You have lived inside your comfort zone for too long and this is stifling your progress and journey. Try something new and face your fears, you will see that you are capable of more than you think you are.

LOVE
Stop holding yourself back where matters of the heart are concerned. Love is in your reach as long as you invite it into your heart.

CAREER
Yes you can make your next step up the career ladder, just believe in yourself then others will.

FINANCES
Invest in yourself.

YES or NO   Yes

Zadkiel brought this message to you.

DREAMS

Pay attention to your dreams as they hold hidden messages for you. Write them down and re-visit them, the messages will become clear.

LOVE
You have been dreaming about what you want in a relationship and it is coming to you so embrace it with open arms.

CAREER
Things are not nearly as bad as they seem, clarity and direction will be available to you if you stand still long enough to see and hear it.

FINANCES
Finances are improving for you and your loved ones, do not forget to treat yourself once in a while, you deserve it.

YES or NO   Yes

Archangel Michael brought this message to you.

NEW BEGINNINGS

New beginnings are starting to happen around you. You will also hear about the birth of a child who will bring you much joy and happiness. This child is a crystal child and will be very spiritual, they will also have fairy-like qualities and will touch the heart of all they meet.

LOVE
This is an exciting time for relationships on all levels, as you will start to see that you are very much loved and respected.

CAREER
Hold on tight! You will be fast tracked into developing new skills and unlocking your true potential. You will also see that your efforts have been noticed and you will be rewarded for your hard work.

FINANCES
Be careful of buying any new electrical items at this time, if you buy cheaply you will need to buy twice!

YES or NO   No

Raphael brought you this message.

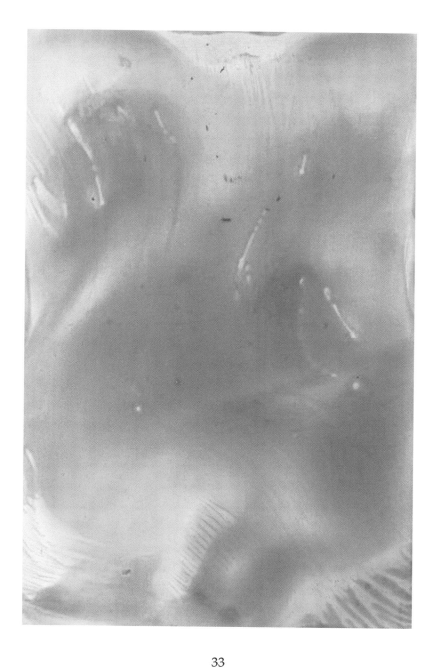

CREATIVITY

Explore your creative side especially where music and art is concerned, you will feel inspired and balanced if you do so.

LOVE
Communication seems to be a problem at the moment within relationships.
You know what you want to say but it does not always reach your mouth. Do not assume that other people around you know what you are thinking.

CAREER
Learn to say No. Someone is asking you to do things that are not your responsibility.

FINANCES
Finances are improving but you cannot spend, spend, and spend just yet.

YES or NO   Yes

Archangel Michael brought this message to you.

THE WIZARD

If you look closely at the image you will see a face of a wizard, turn the page upside down and you will see his face and body. Wizards are able to do magic and make us believe that something is happening when it is only a conjuring trick.

The Angels are asking you to look at things in your life from all angles because what you are seeing and believing to be true; may not be the reality.

LOVE
Is this really what you want? Are you accepting second best? Ask yourself the question and make your decision based on your own answer.

CAREER
Your support and guidance will be needed, give it freely with positive thoughts and you will see you are rewarded for your good deeds.

FINANCES
Your finances are not going to improve unless you take responsibility for your own spending. A complete and honest inventory is needed, once this is done you will be able to move forward and free yourself of debt. Stop kidding yourself.

YES or NO   Yes

Archangel Michael brought this message to you.

FORGIVENESS

Now is the time to forgive others and yourself, as it is holding you back.
Simply imagine the situation or person who you need to forgive surrounded by white light.
You will feel better for letting go of the emotional ties that have bound you for too long.

LOVE
Try not to listen to other peoples' opinions regarding your choices in relationships, you know what you want and so only you can comment.

CAREER
There is an air of jealousy towards you, do not bite back at this time as the person in question will be responsible for their own downfall. You do not need to do anything as the Angels are taking charge of this situation.

FINANCES
Read the small print on any official documents, you may have missed something very important.

YES or NO   No

Archangel Michael brought this message to you.

HELP

Why are you being so stubborn?
You do not have to face this battle alone. Ask for help and you will see that your problems can be overcome.

LOVE
A choice will need to be made, as you seem to have a secret admirer around you.

CAREER
You need to make better use of your time, as you seem to be making little or no progress in the things that need your urgent attention.

FINANCES
Make sure that you do not overstretch yourself financially at this time.

YES or NO   Yes

Archangel Michael brought this message to you.

SENSITIVITY

You are feeling very sensitive at the moment and this is making you point the finger of blame at the wrong person. Do not worry you will be back to your normal state within a matter of days.

LOVE
Do not get into arguments as you may misinterpret what people are saying to you and you will feel that you are being discredited when it really is not the case.

CAREER
You need to do twice as much listening as talking at the moment as you will have a habit of saying the wrong things even though they are well meant.

FINANCES
Open your eyes and you will see that the problems that you think are there have been magnified by your own thinking, if you look closely at the situation you will see that it is not as bad as you think. Swallow your pride and ask for help.

YES or NO   No

Emmanuel brought this message to you.

SURRENDER

The Angels are urging you to stop being hard on yourself. You gave your best and there was nothing more that you could have done.

LOVE
Listen to your heart; it may be time for you to be honest with yourself and move on if this relationship isn't for your highest good.

CAREER
You need to take a break and reassess your career, as your stress levels are high at this time.

FINANCES
Finances are improving over the coming months but the increase will be through work or legal matters and not won.

YES or NO   Yes

Zadkiel brought this message to you.

LIFE PATTERN

You seem to be taking one step forward and one step back in your life at the moment. Learn the lessons and then you can move forward. Ignore them and they will keep re-appearing -The choice is yours.

LOVE
News of an engagement will bring much happiness to all concerned.

CAREER
You will be more prone to losing things at this time. So make sure that you put away important documents safely.

FINANCES
Your finances will be steady and you will see little progress in them until the next season brings about a sense of change.

YES or NO   Yes

Gabriel brought this message to you.

PAST LIFE

You have had many past lifetimes and now is the time to think about what you have learnt in this lifetime as it will hold the key to your future happiness.

LOVE
Do not let feelings of jealousy hinder your relationships. You have no reason to doubt.

CAREER
You chose this career path. Why do you not have the same enthusiasm for it now? Ask yourself what it is that you really want to do?
Remember, you have free will!

FINANCES
There is an old saying, which the Angels want to remind you about.
"Look after the pennies and the pounds will look after themselves".

YES or NO   Yes

Cassiel brought this message to you.

BALANCE

You are spending too much energy on other people and not on yourself.
Your life is out of balance and the Angels are working with you to restore harmony. Ask for their help daily and you will see that miracles will happen for you.

LOVE
Yes, you are loved, even if you don't feel it at the moment. Don't worry; you will feel loved more in the coming weeks.

CAREER
Stop cutting corners and be true to yourself. The only person that you are cheating is YOU!

FINANCES
You are entering a lucky time in your life; money will be coming your way from unexpected sources.

YES or NO   Yes

Camael brought this message to you.

FAMILY

Family matters are important to you at this time. Learn to listen more and you will be able to help younger members around you.

LOVE

You will need to show your support of a loved one, as they are at a crossroads in their life. Draw on your own experiences and life skills to help them.

CAREER

What you want to achieve concerning your career is within your reach.

FINANCES

Seek advice from a professional advisor regarding debts, as you will be able to make some progress in this area.

YES or NO   No

Jophael brought this message to you.

THE ELEMENTS

Your pathway ahead is lit up for you. You are over the worst and any decision you make now will be successful. The Angels are holding your hand to give you the strength to make the next move.

LOVE
Show that you care by physical actions and gifts.

CAREER
Praise is coming your way. Accept it and don't shy away from it as you usually do.

FINANCES
It seems that money is in one hand and out of the other. Patience is needed as the Angels are helping you to receive in abundance.

YES or NO   No

Barakiel brought this message to you.

FAIRY BIRTH

Do you believe in fairies?

The earth elementals are working with you to have more fun. They are concerned that you haven't been laughing recently. Sit quietly in nature and you will see miracles happening all around you. This will give you a greater sense of fun in your life and you will see that people around you are happier too.

LOVE
For the next two months, you will see your love life improving dramatically.

CAREER
You are working too hard at the moment. Don't forget to have some fun.

FINANCES
Invest in hobbies or fitness related issues, as this will give you the drive and determination to achieve the level of financial security that you desire.

YES or NO   No

Zadkiel brought this message to you.

THE UNIVERSE

You will be noticing that you are thinking more about environmental issues. The Universe and Mother Earth is asking you to help. So turn your thoughts into actions.

LOVE
Your social life is expanding as everyone wants to be near you. Make sure that you don't neglect your loved ones at this time, as they need to feel your love.

CAREER
Changes are about to happen which are out of your control. The Angels are telling you that they are for the highest good and that you don't need to worry, as there are blue skies above.

FINANCES
Hold onto your money and don't be tempted by glossy advertisements.

YES or NO   Yes

Gabriel brought this message to you.

CHILDREN

Children will embrace life with wonder. They are not afraid to seek answers to questions. Now is the time to ask your questions to people that you trust and listen to their answers carefully.

LOVE
Quality time is needed. You seem to have drifted apart but it is not too late to recover this relationship if you want to.

CAREER
Business and pleasure certainly don't mix in this instance. Know where your boundaries are and stick to them!

FINANCES
Be careful not to lose money.

YES or NO   Yes

Cassiel brought this message to you.

INSIGHT

You are very wise and you may feel that you need to spend more time on your own with your thoughts. Don't let others try to bully you into doing things that you don't want to. Your spirit guide is showing you that you have strong psychic gifts and you know what is right and what is wrong because you will feel it in your Solar Plexus.

LOVE
A good time for new relationships, which are long lasting.

CAREER
Caution is needed to avoid getting the blame for something that you haven't done.

FINANCES
You will see vast improvements this year regarding finances.

YES or NO   No

Archangel Michael brought this message to you.

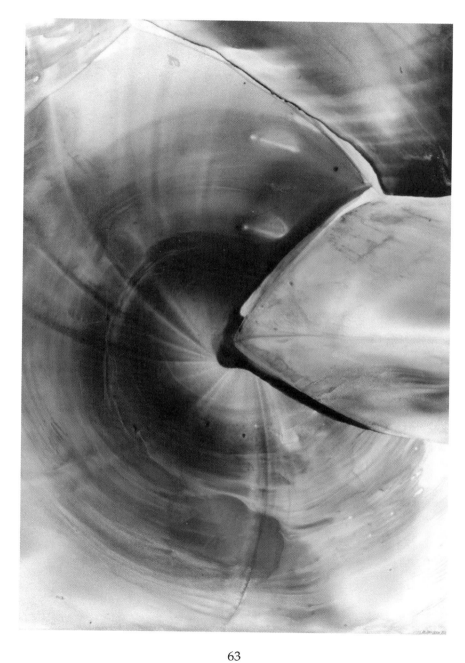

COURAGE

The road ahead may seem to have many twists and turns. Use your own courage and call on your Angels, as they want to help you.

LOVE
Stop worrying and start loving is your message from Archangel Raphael.

CAREER
Look forward to a change in your working conditions. This will bring in many rewards including new friends and rich financial rewards.

FINANCES
Now is a good time to invest in property. Stop dreaming about overseas adventures – Make it happen.

YES or NO   Yes

Raphael brought this message to you.

CRYSTALS

You have a natural affinity with crystals. Place them in your home or wear them to tap into their positive energies and protective qualities.

LOVE
Carry a piece of Rose Quartz to attract the love that you want.

CAREER
More effort is needed if you want to be noticed. Let people know what you are really capable of and you will see that you will get the career you want.

FINANCES
Within the next three months, you will see that you are attracting money towards you. The Universe is giving you a chance to make firm foundations for the future. So don't blow it!

YES or NO   Yes

Israfel brought this message to you.

STRENGTH

You can relax, as you have been the tower of strength for too many people for far too long. The Angels want you to sit back and let others take care of your needs. A loved one who has passed over is sending you messages of thanks as you have been thinking about them recently. They are very proud of you and want to let you know that the gentle breezes that you have felt on your arms is a touch of love from them, just to let you know that they have not left you.

LOVE
You are stronger than you think but you keep falling into a trap of being submissive in relationships. Make sure that your voice is being heard if you want a relationship that is balanced with just the right amount of give and take.

CAREER
You need to be your own boss as you have excellent skills and knowledge. Any new business projects that you start within the next six months will be successful, providing that you do your research properly.

FINANCES
Invest a little in a new project and you will see that money will flow towards you.

YES or NO   No

Cassiel brought this message to you.

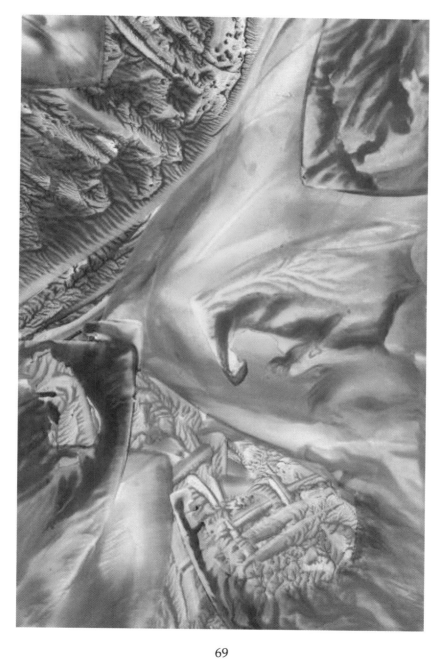

JEALOUSY

People around you are jealous of what you have. Don't get tempted into fighting it with negativity and malice. Simply ask the Angels to sort out the situation for you and you will see good come from it.

LOVE
Start seeing your own qualities. You are worthy of being loved but you never let anyone close enough to see the real you. The Angels know that you have been hurt in the past and are telling you that you will not be hurt in the future.

CAREER
Stay put; don't make any major changes at this time.

FINANCES
You will need to calculate your outgoings as you have missed something and this is draining your resources.

YES or NO   No

Archangel Michael brought this message to you.

DIVINE TIMING

Yes, it will happen but fate has taken a hand here and it will happen in Divine Timing. There is nothing that you can do to rush things, as patience is one of the lessons that you need to learn in this lifetime.

LOVE
Your Soulmate is around you, that is why you feeling such intense feelings about a certain person.

CAREER
Don't make waves by spreading gossip.

FINANCES
Yes, they are improving and you will see this over the coming weeks.

YES or NO   Yes

Cassiel brought this message to you.

ENERGY

Your energy levels are low at the moment. Make some changes to your lifestyle and you will see your energy levels return. Yoga, Meditation or any other relaxation techniques will be beneficial.

LOVE
You know the answer and you are right, so stick with it and see it through. Things will become clearer after the next full moon.

CAREER
Look for new opportunities as these may bring you more security.

FINANCES
You will need to wait a little longer for any major improvement.

YES or NO   Yes

Gabriel brought this message to you.

TRAVEL

Travel to overseas countries will feature very much for you this year. Explore and seek out new cultures as they may bring you a greater understanding of the bigger picture.

LOVE
Yes, they are being truthful.

CAREER
Start making long-term plans for your future, as you have been side tracked.

FINANCES
Explore the options of working for yourself and what financial risks that you may have to take. The Angels and your Spirit Guides will be showing you who to ask for advice.

YES or NO   No

Emmanual brought this message to you.

EMPOWERMENT

You have been thinking about changing your image or surroundings. This will bring you much happiness and greater self-esteem. Do not ask others for advice that you already know the answer to as this will only lead to confusion.

LOVE
A loved one will want to celebrate some good news with you. Don't steal their limelight.

CAREER
Good things are about to happen regarding your career. The Universe is rewarding you for your hard work.

FINANCES
Make sure that you pay back whoever has lent you money to avoid a disagreement.

YES or NO   Yes

Verchiel brought this message to you.

LUCK

You are about to enter one of the luckiest times that you will have this year. You seem to have the Midas touch and any new ventures have a greater chance of succeeding at this time.

LOVE
Love will go from strength to strength. You will be happier than you have been for a long time, so you can stop worrying.

CAREER
People are noticing your key skills so make sure that your self-esteem does not let you down. You are as good as other people think.

FINANCES
Improvement is being made in this area and you will be able to treat yourself within a matter of weeks.

YES or NO   Yes

Tabriss brought this message to you.

NATURE

You need to have a major life clearout. The answers are within nature – clear out the dead wood and watch the new buds appear.
Re-connect with nature by spending time in the fresh air as your spirit has been feeling caged recently and this will help to free it.

LOVE
Without trust, love will not flourish.

CAREER
Yes, you do have the ability to make it a success.

FINANCES
Unexpected expenditure may cause you to worry. Ask the Angels for their help and it will be sorted.

YES or NO   No

Archangel Michael brought this message to you.

OPPORTUNITY

The only person holding you back is YOU! An opportunity is coming your way to have what you want. Don't talk yourself out of it

LOVE
Love will continue to grow, as long as you communicate more.

CAREER
Things are not as bad as they first appear. Wait until you understand the situation fully before making a move.

FINANCES
Someone will make you an offer that you feel you cannot refuse. Listen to your instincts.

YES or NO   No

Raphael brought this message to you.

About the Angels

Angels are there for everyone and communicating with the Angels on a daily basis is a wonderful and magical experience that can enhance our lives.

During the trance sitting for this book a host of Angels came through to give guidance and inspiration.

There are many Angel books available which will give you an insight into each individual Angels. The interpretation of each Angel that is listed below has been channelled from the Angels during the trance sitting and it is in their own words. The words and art throughout this book have not been altered in any way and is a direct transcript of what was channelled through Netty.

Many people spend too much time asking their questions to the Angels and very little time in listening to the answers that the Angels are providing. Remember that the Angels may answer you in a variety of ways ranging from spoken thoughts to physical signs.

Archangel Michael

"I come through on an electric blue ray as this frequency of colour works in harmony with the throat Chakra. Many people have seen me with a golden sword in my hand and although this is true, I also have a gentler energy, which can be felt as a gentle breeze. I will work with you on many levels to achieve your truth."

Colour ray: Electric Blue.

Chakra: Throat.

Key words: Courage, empowerment, and standing in your power.

Crystals: Turquoise.

Meditation to Archangel Michael:
Ground and protect yourself with the white universal light of protection.

Hold a blue crystal in your palm Chakras and breathe into your palms as you ask your question.

Ask Archangel Michael to come close to you and to show you a physical sensation that he is near to you. You may feel this as a gentle touch or change in temperature in the room.

Concentrate on the crystal and listen to the answers that you are receiving.

Thank Archangel Michael for his guidance and support.

Archangel Raphael

"Call on my name when you are going through times when matters of the heart are apparent in your life. It is important to remember that I work for you highest good and when you call on me for assistance I will always answer but I will not necessarily provide you will guidance to the answer that is in your mind. This is because I work with your heart as that is the true pathway to happiness."

Colour ray: Green.

Chakra: Heart.

Key words: Love, truth and integrity.

Crystals: Malachite.

Meditation with Raphael:
Ground and protect yourself with the white universal light of protection.

Hold a green crystal in your palm Chakras and breathe into your palms as you ask your question.

Ask Raphael to come close to you and to show you a physical sensation that he is near to you. You may feel this as a gentle touch or change in temperature in the room.

Bring the crystal to your heart Chakra and hold it there for 5 minutes.

Concentrate on the crystal and listen to the answers that you are receiving.

Thank Raphael for his guidance and support.

Emmanual

"Many people have seen me as I resonate with the white healing light. I work with you to show you direction on your spiritual pathway, giving you guidance and support when you need it most. I also work closely with children as their purity is being corrupted by the thoughts and deeds of many in society. Truth and wisdom will make the way ahead clearer and I will be holding your hand every step of the way. All you have to do is ask me and I will be with you."

Colour ray: White.

Chakra: Crown.

Key words: Insight, Playfulness and Support.

Crystals: Clear Quartz.

Meditation with Emmanual:
Ground and protect yourself with the white universal light of protection.

Lie down and concentrate on your breathing.

Hold a white or clear crystal in your palm Chakras and breathe into your palms as you ask your question.

Ask Emmanual to come close to you and to show you a physical sensation that he is near to you. You may feel this as a gentle touch or change in temperature in the room.

Bring the crystal to your Crown Chakra and hold it there for 5 minutes.

Imagine that the energy from the crystal is penetrating your Crown Chakra.

Concentrate on the crystal and listen to the answers that you are receiving.

Thank Emmanual for his guidance and support.

Camael

"Whenever justice is needed in your life I will be there. I will ensure that the outcome is of benefit to your highest good and that you are able to break free from the ties that have held you back. Many people feel that there is no way of moving forward in their lives but this simply is not true. It is simply because they carry too much baggage with them on their journey. I will help you to realise what you really need and what you do not and by doing so you will be able to move forward as the spiritual being that you are."

Colour ray: Red.

Chakra: Base.

Key words: Justice and Clarity.

Crystals: Bloodstone.

Meditation with Camael:
Ground and protect yourself with the white universal light of protection.

Hold a Red crystal in your palm Chakras and breathe into your palms as you ask your question.

Ask Camael to come close to you and to show you a physical sensation that he is near to you. You may feel this as a gentle touch or change in temperature in the room.

Bring the crystal to your Base Chakra and hold it there for 5 minutes.

Concentrate on the crystal and listen to the answers that you are receiving.

Thank Camael for his guidance and support.

Jophael

"I will appear to you through your dreams giving you guidance as you sleep. I work with the third eye Chakra and with the colour purple to encourage you to listen to your higher self as you have all the answers within you. I work with you to recognise the signs that will give you insight into your life lessons."

Colour ray: Purple.

Chakra: Third eye.

Key words: Vitality, Vision and Harmony.

Crystals: Amethyst.

Meditation with Jophael:
Ground and protect yourself with the white universal light of protection.

Hold a purple crystal in your palm Chakras and breathe into your palms as you ask your question.

Ask Jophael to come close to you and to show you a physical sensation that he is near to you. You may feel this as a gentle touch or change in temperature in the room.

Bring the crystal to your third eye and hold it there for 5 minutes.

Concentrate on the crystal and listen to the answers that you are receiving.

Next take the crystal up to your Crown Chakra. What messages are you getting?

Thank Jophael for his guidance and support.

Gabriel

"I work with the golden hues of the sun and also through the animal kingdoms. Work with me to help you with being the person that you really want to be. Simply ask me a question and tell me what physical sign you would like me to communicate with you through. Maybe you want to see a robin or a white feather as confirmation? Just talk to me."

Colour ray: Gold.

Chakra: Solar Plexus.

Key words: Feelings and Ambition.

Crystals: Tiger Eye.

Meditation with Gabriel:
Ground and protect yourself with the white universal light of protection.

Hold a Tiger Eye crystal in your palm Chakras and breathe into your palms as you ask your question.

Ask Gabriel to come close to you and to show you a physical sensation that he is near to you. You may feel this as a gentle touch or change in temperature in the room.

Bring the crystal to your Solar Plexus Chakra and hold it there for 5 minutes.

Concentrate on the crystal and listen to the answers that you are receiving.

Imagine that your feelings are floating out of your Chakra like a Butterfly.

Thank Gabriel for his guidance and support.

Haniel

"I am working with you to have compassion towards other people. When you see the beauty in others, you own beauty will radiate throughout your very being. When you feel that the world has nothing to offer and those around you have let you down. Ask for my help and I will be there."

Colour ray: Green.

Chakra: Heart.

Key words: Compassion.

Crystals: Rose Quartz.

Meditation with Haniel:
Ground and protect yourself with the white universal light of protection.

Hold a pink or green crystal in your palm Chakras and breathe into your palms as you ask your question.

Ask Haniel to come close to you and to show you a physical sensation that he is near to you. You may feel this as a gentle touch or change in temperature in the room.

Bring the crystal to your heart chakra and hold it there for 10 minutes.

Concentrate on the crystal and listen to the answers that you are receiving.

Any past hurts will surface. When this happens imagine that white light is showing out over them.

Thank Haniel for his guidance and support.

Zadkiel

"I am like the night sky. When you look up at the night sky do you see the darkness and vast space or do you see the stars? I am working with you to receive what is rightfully yours from the universe in abundance. I am also asking for your help to be more mindful of the environment as action is needed now and I am working through various people to help raise awareness of the needs of the earth."

Colour ray: Black and White.

Chakra: Crown.

Key words: Abundance.

Crystals: Tourmalinated Quartz.

Meditation with Zadkiel:
Ground and protect yourself with the white universal light of protection.

Hold a Black and White crystal in your palm chakras and breathe into your palms as you ask your question.

Ask Zadkiel to come close to you and to show you a physical sensation that he is near to you. You may feel this as a gentle touch or change in temperature in the room.

Bring the crystal to your Crown chakra and hold it there for 15 minutes.

Concentrate on the crystal and listen to the answers that you are receiving.

Next bring it to your Third eye chakra and listen to your answers.

Now bring it to your throat chakra.

Thank Zadkiel for his guidance and support.

Matriel

"I am about balance. Remember that when your life is not going the way that you want it to, it is because you need to have both the good and not so good times in your life so that all your lessons can be learnt. Do not see the not so good times as negative times as it is in these times that the greatest lessons can be learnt."

Colour ray: Red.

Chakra: Base.

Key words: Challenge.

Crystals: Any red crystal.

Meditation with Matriel:
Ground and protect yourself with the white universal light of protection.

Hold a Red crystal in your palm Chakras and breathe into your palms as you ask your question.

Ask Matriel to come close to you and to show you a physical sensation that he is near to you. You may feel this as a gentle touch or change in temperature in the room.

Bring the crystal to your Base chakra and hold it there for 5 minutes.

Then bring it to your Crown chakra.

Concentrate on the crystal and listen to the answers that you are receiving.

Thank Matriel for his guidance and support.

Cassiel

"I am helping you with your own empowerment. Why do you seek answers from other people who are too concerned about their own journey? I am here to help you but I will not assist until you ask for me."

Colour ray: Blue and White.

Chakra: Throat.

Key words: Power, Guidance, and Hope.

Crystals: Clear Quartz.

Meditation with Cassiel:
Ground and protect yourself with the white universal light of protection.

Hold the crystal in your palm Chakras and breathe into your palms as you ask your question.

Ask Cassiel to come close to you and to show you a physical sensation that he is near to you. You may feel this as a gentle touch or change in temperature in the room.

As you hold the crystal in your hand you may start to remember times in your life that have been less than straightforward. Ask what lessons you need to learn from them.

Bring the crystal to your base chakra and hold it there for 5 minutes.

Concentrate on the crystal and listen to the answers that you are receiving.

Thank Cassiel for his guidance and support.

Israfel

"I will come through to you on the frequencies of music. If you mediate with music and call my name, I will come to you and help you feel loved and supported. I can see the beauty that you hold in your heart and the beauty of the soul."

Colour ray: Green.

Chakra: Throat and Heart.

Key words: Support, Safety and Creativity.

Crystals: Chrysoprase.

Meditation with Israfel:
Ground and protect yourself with the white universal light of protection.

Hold a green/ blue crystal in your palm Chakras and breathe into your palms as you ask your question.

Ask Israfel to come close to you and to show you a physical sensation that he is near to you. You may feel this as a gentle touch or change in temperature in the room.

Bring the crystal to your heart chakra and hold it there for 5 minutes.

Bring it to your throat chakra and hold it there for 5 minutes.

Concentrate on the crystal and listen to the answers that you are receiving.

Thank Israfel for his guidance and support.

Verchiel

"I will be your rock when you feel that you cannot trust anyone. Call me and concentrate on the Golden colour and I will be with you."

Colour ray: Gold.

Chakra: Solar Plexus.

Key words: Trust and vulnerability.

Crystals: Gold.

Meditation with Verchiel:
Ground and protect yourself with the white universal light of protection.

Lie down and concentrate on your breathing.

Hold an item of gold in your palm Chakras and breathe into your palms as you ask your question.

Ask Verchiel to come close to you and to show you a physical sensation that he is near to you. You may feel this as a gentle touch or change in temperature in the room.

Bring the crystal to your solar plexus chakra and hold it there for 15 minutes.

Concentrate on the gold and then bring it to your throat chakra.

Listen to the answers that you are receiving.

Thank Verchiel for his guidance and support.

Tabriss

"I will help you with changes in your life. You will always see that no matter how hard a change is to make, once it has been made it will always be for the better."

Colour ray: Orange.

Chakra: Sacral.

Key words: Partnerships.

Crystals: Carnelian.

Meditation with Tabriss:
Ground and protect yourself with the white universal light of protection.

Hold an Orange crystal in your palm Chakras and breathe into your palms as you ask your question.

Ask Tabriss to come close to you and to show you a physical sensation that he is near to you. You may feel this as a gentle touch or change in temperature in the room.

Bring the crystal to your sacral chakra and hold it there for 10 minutes.

Imagine that the crystal is changing into a key and unlocking the sacral chakra.

Concentrate on the crystal and listen to the answers that you are receiving.

Thank Tabriss for his guidance and support.

Barakiel

"You are all intuitive and yet you have forgotten how to use this vital gift of life. I can help you rediscover your gifts and use them for your highest sense of purpose."

Colour ray: Purple.

Chakra: Third Eye.

Key words: Enlightenment.

Crystals: Lapis Lazuli.

Meditation with Barakiel:
Ground and protect yourself with the white universal light of protection.

Hold a dark blue or purple crystal in your palm Chakras and breathe into your palms as you ask your question.

Ask Barakiel to come close to you and to show you a physical sensation that he is near to you. You may feel this as a gentle touch or change in temperature in the room.

Gaze into the crystal making a mental note of any changes in sensations or thoughts.

Thank Barakiel for his guidance and support.

Useful Contacts

Isatreya™ Training Ltd
Holistic, Psychic, Angel and Spiritual Training Courses and workshops throughout the UK and Europe.
www.isatreya.com Tel. 0845 22 22 353

Why not have your own personal Angels for Life artwork and interpretation?
Call Netty on 0845 22 22 353

Alexandria™ Connections
A beauty and healing retreat with a difference.
Offering full or half days of inspiring Egyptian style packages for total well-being and relaxation.
www.alexandria-connections.co.uk

Green Designs
An eco interior design company that works in harmony with the environment and uses intuition and guidance from the Angels to help you create the perfect home for the mind, body and spirit.
www.greendesigns.info

Ghias gifts
Wondering what to buy that special someone in your life? Look no further!
Ghia's gifts, provides products inspired by Mother Nature. There is something for everyone at Ghia's gifts so whether you are looking for a special gift for a loved one or are just treating yourself.
www.ghiasgifts.com

Holidays and Retreats

Cottage Isaf is a homely 5 star graded holiday cottage surrounded by fantastic views. Perfect for family holidays, retreats, Dolphin watching and small courses. The cottage is 3 miles from the sandy beach at Llangrannog in Wales and 12 miles from the town of Cardigan. Several stunning beaches along the coastline, where you can watch the Dolphins at play are within easy driving or cycling distance.

www.glyncochisafcottage.co.uk

Has an angel touched your life?

I am currently working on a second Angel book and would like to hear from anyone who has had an Angel experience.

If you have, please write to me at the following address stating a brief outline of your Angelic experience, your name and full contact details:

Netty - Everyday Angels.

C/o Isatreya Training Ltd

145 - 157 St Johns Street

London

EC1V 4PY

Printed in the United States
75343LV00002B